Control Psychology

The Illusionary Game

by

Pankaj Tiwari

Double9 BOOKS

Control Psychology
The Illusionary Game

by Pankaj Tiwari

ISBN: 978-93-63055-25-4

Published by

DOUBLE 9 BOOKS
2/13-B, Ansari Road
Daryaganj, New Delhi – 110002
info@double9books.com
www.double9books.com
Tel. 011-40042856

ABOUT THE AUTHOR

Pankaj Tiwari, born in 2004 in Bihar, discovered his passion for computers at an early age and quickly developed a knack for teaching others. After completing his schooling, he embarked on a journey as a computer teacher, sharing his knowledge and skills with enthusiasm. However, it was during the COVID-19 pandemic that Pankaj's journey took an exciting turn. Seizing the opportunity to learn something new, he delved into coding and found himself immersed in the world of web development. With determination and dedication, Pankaj honed his coding skills and soon began creating impressive websites. His infectious enthusiasm for learning not only propelled his own growth but also inspired those around him to embrace new challenges and pursue their passions Reveal the hidden mechanisms of control psychology and level up your influence game with 'Control Psychology: The Illusionary Game' – where perception meets power.

CONTENTS

Introduction

This book talks about manipulation, which means influencing or controlling others' behaviour. It explains manipulation in a detailed way, breaking it down into smaller parts and giving clear definitions. The book also gives practical advice on how to manipulate others effectively.

In the beginning, it introduces important ideas and explains them well to prepare you for the practical parts of the book later on. It's important to understand that manipulation techniques can vary depending on the situation. Instead of telling you exactly what to do, the book helps you develop your own strategies for manipulation that suit your goals and circumstances.

Examples are included to help you understand how to apply the advice in real-life situations. The book also covers topics like analysis, cold reading, and body language, which are important for forming and executing manipulation strategies.

One key thing the book emphasizes is that manipulation isn't always bad. It addresses ethical issues related to manipulation in a dedicated chapter.

After reading the book, you'll have a better understanding of your own actions and those of others. You'll be equipped with the knowledge of how manipulation works, so you can make informed decisions about when to use it and recognize when others might be manipulating you.

Unlike some other books that promise quick tricks to spot lies or control people easily, this book is honest about its limitations and advises caution when it's appropriate.

What Is Manipulation?

Understanding what manipulation means is really important for this book. It's like setting up the rules so we all understand what we're talking about. If we don't have a clear idea of what manipulation is, it'll be hard to tell when it's happening and when it's just regular influence or persuasion.

You might already have your own idea of what manipulation is, but it's essential to use the definition provided in the book. This way, we're all on the same page and can understand the practical advice given later on.

Basic Ideas

So, when we talk about manipulation in a broad sense, it's about trying to influence how someone behaves or sees things. Most definitions add that manipulation involves using abusive, deceptive, or exploitative methods to differentiate it from other influencing behaviors like persuasion.

Now, let's talk about what "exploitative" means. It's like taking advantage of someone or using them unfairly. Deception is another important aspect. It's when someone hides or changes the truth on purpose. But does deception always mean manipulation? For example, in a job interview, you might not mention the times you were late to work because of hangovers. Is that manipulation? Some would say it's not necessarily dishonest because job interviews are about highlighting your good qualities.

Now, let's put ethics aside for a moment. The word "effort" in the definition of manipulation suggests that even if you try to manipulate someone and fail, it still counts as manipulation. Funny enough, those who are the worst at manipulating often get caught more, so they might get a reputation for being manipulative even if they're not successful.

You might know someone in your life who you think is manipulative. But how do others see them? If they're known as manipulative but still have influence, they might be seen as successful. When thinking about manipulating others, it's important to have clear goals so you can make smart decisions.

At this point, there are more questions than answers. The rest of this chapter will try to clear things up and give a solid definition that will guide us through the rest of the book.

Manipulation Vs Influence

In today's world, we often hear about "influencers" – those people with lots of followers on social media who can sway others' opinions with their posts. The term "influencer" actually comes from the world of advertising. Advertisers noticed that these influencers have the power to get people interested in products, so they started working with them to promote stuff.

Sometimes, influencers tell their followers when they're getting paid to promote something, but other times, they don't. This raises ethical questions, especially if an influencer acts like they just genuinely love a product but are actually being paid by the company that sells it.

It might seem like It would have been easier if advertisers just called these people "manipulators" instead of "influencers." But it's not surprising that they didn't do that. It shows that even though people know advertisers try to influence them, it's still not okay for advertisers to admit it openly. Influencers proudly label themselves as such on their social media profiles, without any negative connotations.

Many influencers, especially those who work with advertisers, have goals that are clearly manipulative. Their main aim is to persuade their followers to buy products so they can make money. It's not always clear if the products they promote are actually beneficial to everyone, or if their followers can afford them. In these situations, the influencer is prioritizing their own interests over others'.

Manipulation doesn't always mean trying to harm others, but it does involve putting your own goals first to some extent. That's an important piece of the puzzle.

It's also helpful to think of "influence" as a broader term that includes manipulation as well as other ways of affecting people, like inspiring them or encouraging them to copy your behaviour.

Manipulation Vs Persuasion

These terms might seem like opposites, with persuasion being seen as the "honest" form of manipulation, where the person is open about their goals and opinions. But for this book's purposes, it's more helpful to think of persuasion as a type of manipulation.

In this view, persuasion is just one way of manipulating someone, which is itself a form of influencing others. Interestingly, persuasion is often not very effective. How many times have you been in an argument with someone only for them to give up and say, "You're right"?

It's relatively easy to persuade someone that smoking is bad for them, but persuading them to actually quit is much harder. If it were easy, governments wouldn't need to put high taxes on tobacco to discourage people from smoking. By this book's definition, the government is trying to manipulate people's behavior by using various methods, including persuasion, to reduce tobacco consumption.

So, besides persuasion, there are other ways to influence people and other methods of manipulation too.

Manipulation typically involves having a purpose and a goal, even if that goal is just causing chaos. Take a great filmmaker, for example. They may influence many people through their work, but they're not setting out to influence others; they're just creating art. People might be inspired or emulate their work, but it's not manipulation.

Another method of manipulation is lying, which is a form of deception. If you lie and someone believes it, their perception will inevitably change. As we've established, whether the manipulation is successful or not, it's still manipulation.

Persuasion, like influence, doesn't have the same negative reputation as manipulation. In fact, being persuasive is often seen as a good thing. But there's a hint of something sinister in phrases like "I can be very persuasive," suggesting a exertion of power over someone else, maybe even abuse. When employers talk about the soft skill of persuasion, it's essentially a polite way of saying manipulation, at least to some extent.

Defining Manipulation

So, to wrap up this chapter, we've come up with a useful definition of manipulation for this book's purposes.

Manipulation is when someone intentionally tries to influence another person's behaviour in order to achieve their own goals. There's no implication that the manipulator's intentions are necessarily bad, and it doesn't specify whether they're acting in the target's best interests or not. It's all possible.

This definition is helpful because it's clear and objective. It doesn't get tangled up in subjective ethical ideas, though that doesn't mean you should ignore your morals.

In this book, you'll learn techniques for manipulation that will help you achieve your goals. That's why persuasion is important too—it can play a big role in manipulation and is closely tied to the advice you'll find here.

There are two remaining problems we need to address. The first one is about "intended influence." It's tricky because it implies responsibility. The truth is, everyone influences others around them all the time, even from a young age. We shouldn't dismiss a child's temper tantrum as not manipulation just because they're too young to understand what they're doing. The same goes for adults who throw tantrums. Intent doesn't always mean conscious behavior; it can also be instinctive. This also acknowledges the existence of people who are naturally good at manipulating others.

The second problem Is the vague ending of the definition: "typically to achieve a goal in the manipulator's interests." It's hard to define "the manipulator's interests," and adding "typically" leaves things too open-ended. This part is only there to create a normalized idea of manipulation for this book's purposes and wouldn't work for a more general definition. After all, how can someone perfectly know their own interests? It's possible to successfully manipulate someone and still end up worse off because of it.

We'll address the latter problem throughout the book whenever it's relevant. Despite its flaws, this definition of manipulation is good enough for the practical parts of the book.

Certainly! Despite these challenges, the definition of manipulation provided is sufficient for the practical aspects of the book. Throughout the chapters, we'll delve deeper into these complexities and provide guidance on how to navigate them effectively.

As we explore various manipulation techniques and strategies, we'll consider the nuances of intent and the diverse interests involved. We'll also examine real-life examples to illustrate how manipulation can manifest in different contexts and how individuals can safeguard themselves against manipulation.

By acknowledging these intricacies and offering practical advice, this book aims to empower readers to recognize manipulation, understand its mechanisms, and make informed decisions in their interactions with others.

Examples of Manipulation

Now that we have a clear definition of manipulation, let's look at some examples. These examples range from everyday situations to more unique or dramatic events. While this book mainly focuses on personal manipulation, the principles are similar whether manipulation happens on an individual level or on a grand scale. However, the methods and complexities of manipulation, like deception, can vary greatly between different contexts, such as conflicts between nations.

In everyday life, examples of manipulation could include:

1. Emotional manipulation: Someone guilt-tripping you into doing something by making you feel bad.
2. Gaslighting: Making you doubt your own perception of reality to gain control over you.
3. Persuasive advertising: Using catchy slogans and appealing visuals to convince you to buy a product.
4. Political propaganda: Spreading misleading information to sway public opinion or gain support for a particular agenda.
5. Economic manipulation: Countries using tariffs or trade restrictions to influence global markets.
6. Psychological warfare: Employing tactics to weaken the morale or will of an opponent during conflicts.

These examples show that manipulation can occur in various forms and contexts, but the underlying principles remain the same. Understanding these examples can help us recognize manipulation and respond effectively in different situations.

Advertising

Even seemingly harmless advertising is actually a form of manipulation according to the definition in this book. Advertising aims to inform you about products or services with the goal of changing your behavior or perception. Some advertising may have positive intentions, like raising money for charities or informing you about genuine savings on a product.

On the more sneaky side, there are advertising methods like influencers who try to influence your buying decisions by making you want to copy their lifestyle. Sometimes online ads blend in with other content, making it hard to tell what's an ad and what's not.

Advertising manipulates by focusing on the good things about a product or service, making it hard to trust ads as unbiased sources of information. Techniques like subliminal advertising even try to plant messages in your mind without you realizing it. You might have heard of famous examples where sexual images or messages are hidden in ads for alcohol, but there are many more subtle ways advertisers try to manipulate us.

Advertising is everywhere, and its goal is often to persuade us to buy something or think a certain way. Here are some common tactics advertisers use to influence us:

1. Emotional appeal: Ads often try to make us feel a certain emotion, like happiness, nostalgia, or fear, to get us to associate those feelings with their product or brand.
2. Bandwagon effect: Advertisers show images of happy people using their product to make us feel like we should join in too and be part of the crowd.
3. Celebrity endorsement: Seeing a celebrity use or endorse a product can make us more likely to want it ourselves, even if we know the celebrity is being paid to promote it.
4. Fear of missing out (FOMO): Ads might create a sense of urgency or scarcity to make us feel like we need to act quickly or we'll miss out on a great deal.
5. Social proof: Ads often include testimonials or reviews from satisfied customers to convince us that their product is worth buying.

These are just a few examples of how advertising can manipulate us into buying things or thinking a certain way. Being aware of these tactics can help us make more informed choices and resist the influence of ads.

Military Strategy

Throughout history, military adversaries have often tried to manipulate each other. This manipulation is expected, especially if you believe in the cause you're fighting for, as it's seen as morally justifiable to use any means to gain an advantage over your enemy.

Let's take a look at an example from history: the Battle of Hastings in 1066 AD. William the Conqueror, a Norman leader, invaded England with his army, which included many mounted knights. Harold Godwinson, the newly crowned King of England, met William's forces near Hastings, by the English Channel. Legend has it that Harold positioned his army atop a hill and waited for the approaching invaders. Seeing the disadvantage of fighting uphill, William ordered a retreat, intending to lure the defenders into pursuing them. This strategy worked, as Harold, sensing victory, chased William's army down the hill, sacrificing their advantageous position in the process. The rest, as they say, is history: William's mounted knights were able to overpower Harold's largely infantry-based army, securing victory and thwarting his only significant opposition in England.

This example illustrates how military leaders strategically manipulate their opponents to gain the upper hand in battle.

While the accuracy of historical accounts may sometimes be questioned, the lesson remains clear: manipulating your enemy can lead to victory. Military leaders throughout history have employed various tactics to outsmart their opponents.

For example, Erwin Rommel, a German general during World War II, was renowned for his tactical brilliance in the North African campaigns against Allied forces, earning him the nickname "the Desert Fox." His strategies often involved obstructing or distorting the information received by his adversaries, similar to how you would manipulate another person.

You can also see parallels in games like chess and real-time strategy video games, where successful strategies often rely on deceiving your opponents about your intentions.

In essence, whether on the battlefield or in a game, the art of manipulation can play a crucial role in achieving victory.

The Professional World

In the professional world, encountering ambitious individuals aiming to climb the corporate ladder is quite common. Here, a certain level of manipulation is expected. This dynamic can become complicated, especially when working with personal friends, as it involves managing both competitive and supportive relationships simultaneously.

In professional settings, you encounter various relationship dynamics. Your interactions with fellow team members differ from those with your boss or subordinates. Nowadays, corporate structures tend to be flatter, and managers rely less on authority alone. Instead, they focus on motivating their employees. It's worth noting that motivation can also be seen as a form of manipulation.

This book focuses on both professional and personal relationships, so you can expect relevant examples of manipulation in the workplace.

In the workplace, manipulation can manifest in various ways, such as:

1. Office politics: Employees may engage in manipulation to gain favor or advance their own agendas within the organization.
2. Performance reviews: Managers may use feedback or performance evaluations as a means of manipulating employees to meet certain goals or expectations.
3. Negotiations: Manipulation can occur during negotiations, where parties may use tactics to gain an advantage or secure a favourable outcome.
4. Team dynamics: Manipulation may also occur within teams, where individuals may try to influence others to support their ideas or projects.
5. Promotions and career advancement: Employees may engage in manipulation to position themselves favorably for promotions or career opportunities within the company.

Understanding these dynamics can help individuals navigate the complexities of workplace relationships and make informed decisions in their professional lives.

Personal Relationships

Personal relationships, including family, friendships, and romantic partnerships, are natural breeding grounds for manipulation, despite being the most controversial arena for it. Interestingly, manipulation is often innate and instinctive, starting from the moment we're born. Babies cry to communicate their immediate needs, like hunger or discomfort, and to receive care and attention.

Manipulation in personal relationships can spark controversy because it's sometimes viewed as unnatural and rooted in a desire for control. However, there's a gray area here. For example, it's common for parents to influence their child's behavior through a system of rewards and punishments. This is typically seen as part of a child's upbringing and a healthy aspect of their development, preparing them for adulthood.

Manipulation in a romantic relationship often carries negative connotations. It brings to mind images of someone lying or emotionally manipulating their partner to hide their behavior or trap them in a relationship. However, there's a flip side to this. Some people might actually praise manipulation, even if it involves deceit, if the ultimate goal is to help their partner quit smoking or lose weight.

These ethical questions will be discussed later in the book. For now, it's helpful to think about the different situations where manipulation might be present. Take a moment to observe the world around you and identify examples of manipulation, understanding how they work and the effects they can have.

It's Important to recognize that manipulation in romantic relationships can take many forms, ranging from subtle persuasion to outright deception. While some manipulation tactics may be seen as morally questionable, others may be perceived as well-intentioned efforts to improve the relationship or help a partner make positive changes.

As you navigate the complexities of personal relationships, it's essential to be mindful of the dynamics at play and to communicate openly and honestly with your partner. By fostering trust and mutual respect, you can build a strong foundation for a healthy and fulfilling relationship.

In the upcoming chapters of the book, we'll delve deeper into the ethical considerations surrounding manipulation and explore strategies for navigating these challenges in various aspects of life.

Advantages of Manipulation

This chapter is short but straightforward. The benefits of manipulation are clear, much like the benefits of bank robbery. Successfully manipulating others is a way to influence the world around you and shape it according to your desires. While this might sound sinister, it's highly likely that you're already engaging in manipulation to some extent.

To distinguish between what you might already be doing and what you can learn from this book, interpret this chapter as highlighting the advantages of consciously, deliberately, and effectively manipulating others. In other words, it's about understanding how to use manipulation as a tool to achieve your goals in a strategic and ethical manner.

Recognizing that manipulation is a part of human interaction, this chapter emphasizes the importance of understanding its mechanisms and harnessing its power for constructive purposes. By becoming more aware of how manipulation works and learning effective strategies, you can enhance your ability to influence others positively and achieve your objectives.

While manipulation often carries negative connotations, it's essential to acknowledge its potential benefits when used ethically and responsibly. Throughout this book, you'll explore practical techniques and insights to refine your manipulation skills, empowering you to navigate various situations more effectively and achieve success in both personal and professional endeavors.

Achieve Your Goals

By successfully manipulating others, you can influence their behavior, their opinions, and even their goals to serve your own interests. It's as straightforward as that.

However, effective manipulation goes beyond just influencing others; it's about increasing your chances of success. For example, imagine several coworkers vying for a promotion. While hard work is important, it might not be enough on its own. You need to find ways to make your boss want to promote you specifically. Understanding this concept gives you an advantage.

Similarly, it's one thing to express your feelings to your crush, but it's another to become the object of their desire. Effective manipulation involves creating a situation where your success becomes the most likely or even inevitable outcome.

Mastering the art of manipulation isn't about deceit or coercion but rather about skillfully navigating social dynamics to achieve your desired outcomes. It's about understanding human behavior and using that knowledge to create situations where people naturally gravitate towards supporting your goals.

In the workplace, this might involve positioning yourself as a valuable asset to your team or demonstrating leadership qualities that make you stand out to your superiors. Similarly, in personal relationships, effective manipulation could mean fostering an environment where your partner sees you as the ideal companion.

Ultimately, the key to successful manipulation lies in building trust, fostering genuine connections, and aligning your interests with those of the people you seek to influence. By approaching manipulation with integrity and empathy, you can enhance your ability to navigate various social scenarios and achieve your desired outcomes.

Help Others

If you believe in a cause, you can use manipulation to help it succeed. This could involve various actions, like setting up a swear jar to discourage a family member from cursing or rallying support for your political party.

In essence, it's similar to pursuing your own goals, but instead, you're prioritizing the interests of someone or something else. As the definition states, manipulation is a type of influence, and by employing it for a cause, you're working to shape outcomes in favor of that cause.

By employing manipulation in support of a cause, you're essentially leveraging your ability to influence others to benefit that cause. Whether it's encouraging people to adopt certain behaviors, donate to a charity, or advocate for a particular issue, manipulation can be a powerful tool for driving positive change.

However, it's important to approach manipulation for a cause with integrity and sincerity. This means being transparent about your intentions and ensuring that the methods you use are ethical and aligned with the values of the cause you're supporting. By doing so, you can maximize the impact of your efforts and contribute to meaningful outcomes.

Guard Yourself Against the Manipulation of Others

The more you know about manipulation, the better prepared you'll be to avoid falling victim to it. When you can identify manipulative behaviors in others, you not only shield yourself from their influence but also gain insight into their intentions, providing you with valuable information that you can use to influence them in return.

While it's relatively easy to recognize situations where manipulation might occur, it's more challenging to always spot when you're being manipulated yourself. This requires understanding the goals of others and how they're trying to achieve them in any given situation. With this knowledge, you can not only identify and respond to others' behavior but also anticipate their future actions.

Developing this skill requires emotional intelligence, which involves putting yourself in the shoes of the person trying to manipulate you. Start by assessing your own behavior objectively and understanding your choices from a neutral standpoint. Although it may take some practice, later chapters will delve into this topic in more detail.

Understanding manipulation also involves recognizing your own actions and motivations. By objectively assessing your behavior, you can gain insights into how others might perceive and respond to you. This self-awareness is crucial for navigating interpersonal dynamics effectively and avoiding inadvertently manipulating others.

As you become more adept at identifying manipulative tactics, you'll also develop the ability to predict the future actions of those trying to influence you. This predictive skill is valuable in staying one step ahead and maintaining control over your own decisions and actions.

While learning to recognize manipulation and its underlying motivations takes practice, the knowledge gained from understanding these dynamics empowers you to navigate social interactions more confidently and ethically. In subsequent chapters, you'll delve deeper into strategies for both recognizing and responding to manipulation effectively.

Manipulation Fundamentals

Now that you have a solid foundation from the early chapters, it's time to delve into some crucial aspects of manipulating others. With this groundwork, you can better understand the ideas presented in this chapter and grasp effective approaches to manipulation.

In the Methodology chapter, you'll learn how to apply these ideas to form a coherent strategy. This strategy will enhance your ability to successfully manipulate others and achieve your goals.

Goals Your Goals

Given that you're likely already influencing the people around you to some extent, and being influenced yourself, the first important step in effective manipulation is understanding and defining your goals. Without clear goals, it's impossible to assess how effective your manipulation efforts are.

However, it doesn't mean you aren't already manipulating to some degree. Some people are naturally more inclined to manipulate, while others may not realize they're doing it.

Start by reflecting on your interactions and behavior with others. Think about who you admire or respect at work or in your social circle, and who you might view negatively. Consider if your behavior aligns with your opinion of them. You might find that you're already trying to impress those you perceive as having power or influence.

This is a common approach in society. For example, you might behave differently around your boss compared to your coworkers, regardless of your personal feelings towards them.

Understanding your goals in manipulation is crucial because it helps you focus your efforts and evaluate your effectiveness. For instance, if your goal is to gain a promotion, you might adjust your behavior around your superiors to make a favorable impression.

Once you've defined your goals, you can start thinking about how to achieve them through manipulation. This might involve tactics like building rapport, subtly influencing others' perceptions, or strategically withholding information.

Remember, manipulation isn't inherently negative. It's a tool that can be used for both good and bad purposes. The key is to be aware of your intentions and the potential impact of your actions on others.

Defining your goals is like setting a destination on a map before starting a journey. Your goal could be something specific, like aiming for a certain job position, or it could be more general, like trying to impress others or make your work easier. You might even have personal goals, like getting closer to a colleague you're interested in romantically.

Take some time at the end of each day to reflect on what you've been focusing on and what you've been trying to achieve. This will help you understand your natural motives and desires better.

Once you have a clear goal in mind, it's important to make it specific and measurable. Instead of just aiming to "do well at work," set a goal like "earn a raise" or "achieve a salary of $X per year by MM/DD/YY." Having a deadline adds extra motivation to avoid failure.

With a defined goal, you can evaluate your actions more effectively. Ask yourself, "Will this action help me achieve X?" This can guide you in making smarter decisions aligned with your objectives.

But before you start changing your behavior, there are some important things to consider. Keep an eye out for unexpected challenges or obstacles that might arise along the way.

Imagine defining your goals as setting sail on a voyage. You need a clear destination, like a treasure island on the horizon. Your goal might be the treasure itself, but you also need to know exactly where it is and when you plan to reach it.

Think of your goals like planting seeds in a garden. You need to know what you want to grow and where you want it to flourish. Whether it's a towering oak or a bed of roses, each seed represents a specific goal, and you must nurture it with care and attention.

Once you've planted your seeds, you'll need to tend to them regularly. Water them with effort, nourish them with determination, and shield them from the weeds of distraction and doubt.

As your garden of goals begins to sprout, you'll find yourself walking along a path lined with possibilities. Each step you take brings you closer to the lush oasis of success you've envisioned.

But beware of the storms that may roll in unexpectedly, threatening to uproot your dreams. Stay vigilant, keep your compass pointed towards your objectives, and navigate through the turbulent waters with resilience and determination.

The Goals of Others

Think of manipulation as a game of chess. Your goals are like your pieces on the board, guiding your moves and strategies. However, to win the game, you must also understand your opponent's pieces and their moves. In manipulation, your opponent's goals are crucial pieces of information that can help you make your next move wisely.

Imagine you're trying to convince your friend to go to a particular restaurant for dinner. Your goal is to enjoy a delicious meal there. However, your friend's goal might be to save money or eat something healthy. To manipulate the situation in your favor, you would need to understand your friend's goal and find a way to align it with yours. You might highlight the restaurant's affordable options or its healthy menu choices, appealing to your friend's desire to save money or eat healthily.

In this way, manipulation involves using the goals of others to achieve your own objectives, much like strategically maneuvering your pieces on a chessboard to outsmart your opponent and win the game.

Think of yourself as a valuable piece in a puzzle. Your skills and abilities can help others achieve their goals, just like fitting the right puzzle piece into its place.

For instance, imagine a colleague is tasked with organizing a business trip to an important trade expo. Their success at the expo is crucial for their career advancement. If they believe your skills will contribute to the success of the trip, they're likely to bring you along. This opportunity not only benefits them but also boosts your own value as an employee, potentially putting you in line for a promotion.

Similarly, consider if your employer aims to increase profits by expanding your division. If your division is doing well or there's a growing market for your services, they may need more workers, like crane operators in a construction company. If you happen to be an experienced crane operator, your boss might prefer giving you a raise rather than hiring and training someone new, saving time and money in the process.

In both scenarios, your skills and contributions align with the goals of others, making you a valuable asset in achieving success.

In these examples, your ability to help others achieve their goals enhances your value to them. It's like being the key that unlocks a door for someone else's success.

Imagine you're part of a team working on a project. If your expertise is crucial for the project's success, your team members are more likely to rely on you and support your ideas. This not only benefits the project but also strengthens your position within the team.

Similarly, in personal relationships, understanding and supporting your partner's goals can strengthen your bond and mutual trust. If you help your partner achieve their goals, they'll likely reciprocate, creating a positive cycle of support and cooperation.

Overall, recognizing how your goals align with those of others can help you navigate relationships and situations more effectively, ultimately leading to mutual benefits and success. It's like finding common ground where everyone wins.

In these scenarios, you're not manipulating anyone yet; you're just figuring out how your goals fit with theirs. However, the manipulation comes in when you start shaping situations to align their actions with your goals.

Now, let's talk about romantic relationships. If you're interested in someone romantically, your main goal might be to start a relationship with them. But things can get complicated because it's not always clear what someone wants from a relationship, even to themselves. Many people haven't thought deeply about why they're attracted to others. So, if you want to manipulate the situation effectively to start a relationship, you might need to understand that person better than they understand themselves.

For now, just think about this idea as something to consider.

Imagine you're trying to figure out how to start a romantic relationship with someone you like. It's not just about what you want; it's also about understanding what they want, even if they're not sure themselves. So, effective manipulation in this situation means knowing them better than they know themselves. It's about guiding the situation to align with your desired outcome, all while respecting their feelings and desires.

Actions

Actions are simply the things people do. They include everything from facial expressions and body movements to what people say and the decisions they make. Even acts of violence or sabotage are actions. By observing someone's actions, we can understand their behavior better. When actions are repeated, they form patterns that help us recognize certain behaviors.

Think of actions as the building blocks of behavior, like pieces in a puzzle that come together to form a picture of someone's personality and intentions. Just as each piece in a puzzle contributes to the overall image, each action contributes to understanding someone's behavior. Whether it's a smile, a gesture, or a decision made under pressure, each action reveals a part of the larger picture. And just like putting together a puzzle, observing these actions helps us see the complete picture more clearly.

Tools

Think of goals as the destination you want to reach, and tools as the means to get there. Just like a carpenter uses tools like a hammer and nails to build a house, you use tools to influence others and achieve your goals. These tools could be anything from persuasive language to strategic actions. By understanding your goals and having the right tools at your disposal, you can effectively shape the actions of others to align with your objectives.

Imagine your goals as the treasure you're seeking, hidden deep within a labyrinth. Now, think of your tools as the map and compass guiding you through the twists and turns, helping you navigate toward that treasure. In this book, persuasion isn't just a method; it's like a trusty tool kit, filled with everything you need to navigate the maze of human interaction and reach your desired destination.

Power

In the previous part about Goals, you learned about scenarios at work where you could assist others in reaching their objectives. This ability gives you power or influence in those situations.

Power is the ability to help other people succeed.

The definition of power here flips the usual understanding of forceful control over others. It suggests that having power can also mean helping others succeed by not causing harm or hindrance. Essentially, it's about the ability to influence outcomes, whether positively or negatively.

Consider what you offer people to aid them in achieving their goals. Special talents or skills are a clear example. Whether it's excelling in sports, business, or parenting, if you possess talents others can benefit from, that's a form of power.

Another type of power is authority. For instance, a boss decides who gets promoted or fired, while a police officer can make arrests or issue warnings due to their sanctioned authority. Similarly, judges have the power to determine sentences based on certain rules and their judgment of a person's character.

However, there's a challenge: You might have the same or even better talents than someone else, yet they might be more successful or respected.

Imagine talents and authority as tools in a toolbox. Some people have a shiny, impressive hammer, while others possess a sturdy wrench. Both are valuable, but they serve different purposes. However, sometimes, despite having a top-notch tool, someone else might still build a better house. It's like having a powerful engine in a car, but someone else driving a similar model wins the race because they know the track better.

Success isn't just about having the right tools; it's also about knowing how to use them effectively. Just as a skilled carpenter can create wonders with simple tools, mastering your talents and understanding your authority can lead to remarkable achievements. So, it's not just about possessing power; it's about wielding it wisely to shape your destiny.

Think of reputation as your shadow – it follows you everywhere, influencing how others perceive you. If your shadow is big and strong, people will likely see you as powerful and capable. Your reputation is like a mirror reflecting how others see you. If they believe you're skilled and trustworthy, they'll be more inclined to listen to you and follow your lead.

In the game of manipulation, reputation is like currency. The more respected and admired you are, the easier it is to sway others to your way of thinking. So, while having talents and authority is essential, it's your reputation that truly amplifies your power.

Persuasion

Think of persuasion as a gentle nudge to get someone to do something differently. It's like convincing a friend to try a new restaurant or convincing your parents to extend your curfew. Persuasion is all about using words and reasons to change someone's mind or behavior. It's like being a smooth talker who can make others see things from your perspective.

Persuasion is the effort to convince another person to change their actions

Persuasion involves presenting your ideas or arguments in a way that makes them appealing or convincing to others. It's like being a skilled storyteller who can weave a narrative that captivates you're audience and influences their decisions. Whether you're trying to sell a product, win an argument, or rally support for a cause, persuasion is about using language and reasoning to sway someone's opinion or behavior in your favor.

Persuasion, on its own, can be challenging because people often see through the attempt to convince them, especially if they suspect you have something to gain. It's like trying to sell ice to Eskimos—they know they already have plenty, so they're not easily persuaded.

Persuasion works best when you can offer new information that changes someone's perspective or when they believe your goals align positively with theirs. It's like shedding light on a dark path, guiding them toward a better understanding or a shared vision.

However, when you lack genuine information or trust, persuasion alone may not be enough. That's when deception comes into play, like dressing a wolf in sheep's clothing. You're still trying to persuade, but this time by hiding the truth or bending it to your advantage.

In such situations, persuasion becomes more effective when combined with other tactics, like deception. This means you might need to weave a convincing tale, painting a picture that aligns with their interests, even if it's not entirely truthful. It's like crafting a masterpiece, using every brushstroke to create an illusion that serves your purpose.

Ultimately, the effectiveness of persuasion depends on how well you can manipulate the information available to you and tailor it to the desires and beliefs of the other party. It's like playing a strategic game of chess, where every move is calculated to influence the outcome in your favor.

Deception

The third tool for manipulation is called "**emotional appeal**." It's like adding a dash of spice to a dish, making it more enticing and appealing. Emotional appeal involves tapping into people's feelings and emotions to influence their decisions or actions.

Imagine you're trying to convince someone to support a cause. Instead of bombarding them with facts and figures, you appeal to their emotions by telling a heartwarming story or showing them images that evoke empathy and compassion. This emotional connection can sway their opinion and motivate them to take action.

Emotional appeal is powerful because it speaks directly to people's hearts, bypassing their rational thinking. It's like playing a beautiful melody that resonates with the listener's soul, stirring up deep-seated emotions and driving them to act in a certain way.

When used effectively, emotional appeal can be a potent tool for manipulation, guiding people's behavior in line with your goals. However, it's essential to use it ethically and responsibly, ensuring that you're not manipulating others for selfish or harmful purposes.

Deception is the control of information.

Thinking objectively means looking at things without bias or emotion. It's like seeing the world through clear glasses, where you focus on facts and logic rather than feelings or personal opinions. When you start thinking objectively, you can imagine people as machines, programmed to achieve goals by reacting to information and taking actions based on that input.

Imagine each person as a machine with a goal, and the information they receive as the fuel that drives their actions. If you control the information they receive, you can manipulate their actions by deceiving them. Deception plays a central role in manipulation because it's crucial for the people you manipulate to believe that their actions benefit them. Otherwise, they wouldn't have any reason to act in a certain way. The goal of deception is to control information in a way that leads them to take actions that serve your interests.

However, deception comes with risks. The main danger is being discovered, which can lead to consequences. That's why it's best to avoid deception when possible, and if used, it should be carefully managed. An ideal deception minimizes risk and maximizes reward, with plausible deniability if caught. There's also the risk that one lie leads to another, creating a web of deceit that can spiral out of control. So, what may seem like a good idea at first can turn into a terrible decision if not handled carefully.

Deception in manipulation is like playing a delicate game of chess. You carefully strategize your moves, anticipating your opponent's reactions, and always staying several steps ahead. However, just like in chess, one wrong move can lead to your downfall.

Imagine each lie as a piece on the chessboard. You place them strategically, hoping to control the game and steer it in your favor. But if your opponent sees through your deception, it's like they've uncovered your strategy and are ready to counterattack.

That's why it's crucial to tread carefully with deception. You want to maintain control over the situation without raising suspicion. It's a balancing act between achieving your goals and avoiding the pitfalls of being discovered.

Ultimately, successful manipulation requires a mastery of deception. It's about knowing when to use it, how to use it, and when to back off to avoid the risks. Like a skilled chess player, you must think several moves ahead and anticipate every possible outcome before making your move.

Irrational Behavior

Imagine each person as a puzzle with different pieces representing their goals. Sometimes, it might seem like someone's missing a piece or putting it in the wrong place, making their actions confusing. But in reality, they might just have a different picture in mind for their puzzle.

For example, let's say a colleague at work isn't putting in much effort and seems more interested in socializing than getting ahead in their career. At first glance, it might seem irrational, but maybe their main goal isn't career advancement. Perhaps they prioritize having fun or building relationships at work over climbing the corporate ladder.

In manipulation, we don't judge whether someone's goals make sense to us. Instead, we focus on understanding their puzzle and using that knowledge to predict and influence their future actions. Their goals might not align with what we expect, but as long as we understand what drives them, we can manipulate the situation to our advantage.

In the realm of manipulation, what matters most is understanding the pieces of each person's puzzle – their goals – and using that understanding to navigate the situation. Whether their goals seem rational or not is beside the point; what's crucial is recognizing how those goals drive their behavior.

Consider it like trying to solve a mystery. Each person has their own clues and motivations, and it's up to us to piece them together to uncover their intentions. Once we understand what drives them, we can tailor our approach to manipulate the situation in our favor.

So, next time you encounter someone whose actions seem puzzling, remember that they're just operating with a different set of puzzle pieces. By understanding their goals, you can manipulate the situation to achieve your own objectives, regardless of whether their goals seem rational to you.

Irrational behaviour is a cognitive failure to perform actions which help achieve one's goals.

Goals as the guiding stars of a person's journey. These stars shine bright, leading them toward their desired destination. But sometimes, what seems like a clear path may actually be veiled in fog, hiding the true intentions behind their actions.

In our example, someone may declare their intention to reach the summit of career success as the head of sales. But if their actions don't align with this ambition, it's like they're navigating blindly, stumbling through the fog without a clear direction. Their stated goal may shine brightly, but their true path remains obscured.

Irrational behavior, on the other hand, is like taking a detour off the beaten path, driven more by impulse than reason. It's akin to rolling the dice in a lottery, hoping for a stroke of luck despite knowing the odds are stacked against you. Despite the rational knowledge that the chances of success are slim, the allure of the prize draws people in, like moths to a flame.

So, when trying to decipher someone's actions, it's essential to look beyond their stated goals and navigate through the fog of irrational behavior to uncover their true motivations.

Social media platforms employ a clever tactic, akin to dangling a carrot in front of a horse, to keep users hooked: the endless scroll. It's like walking through a vast garden with each step revealing a new flower, tempting you to keep wandering in search of that one rare bloom. Users keep scrolling, hoping to stumble upon something captivating amidst the sea of mundane content.

This continuous scrolling feeds into our innate desire for novelty and excitement, tapping into the same thrill-seeking impulse that drives people to play the lottery. Just as each pull of the lever offers a chance at a jackpot, each swipe of the screen holds the promise of discovering something intriguing.

However, not everyone is equally susceptible to these manipulative tactics. Just as some travelers may resist the allure of the garden's endless paths, some users may be more resistant to the addictive pull of social media feeds.

But here's the twist: even irrational behavior follows a pattern, like a dancer moving to an unpredictable rhythm. While it may seem random at first glance, a closer look often reveals a method to the madness. This unpredictability makes irrational behavior just as valuable as rational behavior in understanding and influencing others.

So, in the dance of manipulation, it's crucial to keep an eye out for those unexpected steps and incorporate them into your strategy. Just as a skilled dancer adapts to the changing beat, a savvy manipulator adjusts their approach to account for both rational and irrational behavior.

Understanding irrational behavior is like navigating through a maze where the walls keep shifting. Just when you think you've found your way, a new twist throws you off course. But rather than seeing it as an obstacle, savvy manipulators view it as an opportunity—a chance to uncover hidden motivations and shape outcomes in their favor.

Imagine you're playing a game of chess against an opponent who moves their pieces unpredictably. While their strategy may seem haphazard, there's often a method to their madness. By observing their moves and anticipating their next steps, you can use their irrational behavior to your advantage, guiding the game toward your desired outcome.

Similarly, in the realm of manipulation, recognizing and capitalizing on irrational behavior is like finding a secret passage in the maze. It's a shortcut to achieving your goals, bypassing the usual obstacles and pitfalls along the way.

So, whether your target is swiping through a social media feed or making decisions in the workplace, remember to keep an eye out for those unexpected twists and turns. By understanding the irrational side of human behavior, you can unlock new pathways to success and outmaneuver even the most unpredictable opponents.

Manifestations of Manipulation

Approaches to manipulation are like different strategies in a game of chess, each designed to outmaneuver your opponent and achieve victory. These approaches involve using the tools we've discussed—power, persuasion, and deception—in clever ways to influence the actions of others.

Imagine you're a skilled painter with a palette full of colors. Each color represents a different approach to manipulation, and you can mix and match them to create the perfect masterpiece. From subtly persuading a friend to see things your way to orchestrating a complex scheme to influence a whole organization, the possibilities are endless.

In your everyday life, you might already be using these approaches without even realizing it. For example, when you subtly drop hints to sway a group decision or strategically withhold information to gain an advantage, you're employing manipulation tactics.

By examining these approaches, you can gain a deeper understanding of how manipulation works and how you can use it to navigate social situations and achieve your goals. Just remember, like a skilled artist, it's essential to use your tools wisely and ethically to create the desired outcome.

The Carrot and the Stick

The "carrot and stick" approach to manipulation is like dangling a tempting carrot in front of someone to encourage them to move in a certain direction, while also wielding a stick to deter them from undesirable actions. It's a classic method used to influence behavior, seen in families, schools, and workplaces worldwide.

Think of it as a form of justice—rewarding good behavior with a carrot (a positive outcome or reward) and punishing bad behavior with a stick (a negative consequence or punishment). It's something humans naturally do to maintain order and encourage desirable actions.

In personal relationships, you might use this approach without even realizing it. For example, if your partner helps with household chores, you might reward them with affection and be more willing to do something nice for them in return. But if they neglect their responsibilities, you might express your displeasure or withhold affection as a form of punishment.

Just like using a carrot and stick to guide a stubborn mule, this approach involves offering incentives to encourage desired behavior and applying consequences to deter undesirable actions. It's a way of nudging people in the direction you want them to go, whether it's to promote harmony in a relationship or achieve goals in other areas of life.

In workplaces, bosses often motivate employees with bonuses and the looming threat of losing their job if they underperform. But what about interactions among colleagues? If a coworker's actions benefit your work or make it easier, it's natural to acknowledge and encourage that behavior. Conversely, if they create extra problems for you, it can strain your relationship, leading to tension or avoidance.

This dynamic exists in all relationships. However, when you're trying to influence people, you might find that your actions don't always produce the desired outcome. For instance, if you thank Jeff for his help, but then he fails to assist you later, it could be because he prioritized someone else's needs over yours.

Imagine Jeff has to choose between helping you or Bill, who ignored him after a previous incident. If Jeff expects to receive cold treatment from Bill again, he might choose to prioritize Bill's needs to avoid facing consequences, even if it means missing out on your appreciation ("carrot"). This illustrates how people weigh their options and make calculated decisions based on past experiences and potential outcomes.

In essence, the carrot-and-stick approach reflects the balance of incentives and consequences in human interactions. It's about rewarding desirable behavior and discouraging undesirable actions. However, in complex social dynamics, the effectiveness of this approach can vary.

For example, in a team setting, publicly acknowledging and appreciating a colleague's efforts can motivate them to continue performing well. Conversely, ignoring or criticizing their contributions may lead to resentment and reduced cooperation.

Similarly, if someone consistently fails to meet expectations, applying consequences such as assigning them less desirable tasks or providing constructive feedback can encourage improvement. However, if these consequences are perceived as unjust or disproportionate, they may backfire and damage morale or trust within the team.

Ultimately, successful manipulation through the carrot-and-stick method requires a nuanced understanding of individual motivations, interpersonal dynamics, and the careful calibration of incentives and consequences to elicit the desired behaviors.

What just happened is you tried to influence the situation, but it didn't work as planned. You thanked Jeff, but it didn't lead to the desired outcome.

Let's break it down:

1. Your ability to help Jeff was seen as less influential than another person's ability to create obstacles for him.
2. Your attempt to convince Jeff of your influence didn't work because you didn't provide convincing information.
3. Since you didn't use deception, Jeff ended up with more work.

There could be a few reasons for this. Maybe Jeff responds better to avoiding conflict than seeking rewards. Or he might think that Bill has more power than you do, meaning Bill can help him more with his goals. Perhaps Jeff believes that Bill has a better career path or more influence in the office.

This doesn't mean that punishment always works better than rewards. You might find that someone like Ted prefers rewards and doesn't respond well to criticism. The key is to understand what motivates people and what their goals are.

Understanding what drives people and what they aim to achieve is crucial in influencing their actions effectively.

For example, let's say you want to persuade your friend to join you in a new project. You might offer them the opportunity to lead a crucial aspect of the project as a reward. However, if they perceive that another friend has more influence or offers a better opportunity, they might decline your offer, regardless of the reward you're offering.

In such cases, it's essential to reassess your approach and adapt your strategy accordingly. You might need to find ways to increase your perceived value or appeal to different motivations to sway their decision in your favor.

Remember, manipulation isn't always about deceit or coercion; it's about understanding human behavior and using that knowledge to achieve desired outcomes.

Emotional Manipulation

Emotional intelligence plays a big role in how people influence each other. When it comes to manipulation, emotional tactics often come into play. These methods work alongside other tools to shape how others behave.

Emotional manipulation isn't necessarily about pushing someone to act irrationally. Instead, it usually involves distorting the truth or altering someone's perception of reality to steer them toward certain actions that benefit the manipulator's goals.

Imagine someone painting a picture of a situation in a way that makes others feel a certain way or see things differently. It's like creating a new landscape in their minds, leading them down a path they might not have taken otherwise. Emotional manipulation can be subtle but powerful, guiding people's decisions without them even realizing it.

Another aspect of emotional manipulation is exploiting someone's vulnerabilities or playing on their emotions to gain an advantage. This could involve using guilt, fear, or affection to influence their actions.

For example, a salesperson might use emotional manipulation by appealing to a customer's insecurities to convince them to buy a product. They might create a sense of urgency or make the customer feel like they're missing out if they don't make a purchase right away.

Similarly, in personal relationships, someone might use emotional manipulation to control their partner's behavior by making them feel guilty or insecure about certain aspects of themselves or the relationship.

Overall, emotional manipulation can be subtle and insidious, often leaving the manipulated person feeling confused or unsure about their own feelings and motivations. It's important to be aware of these tactics and to approach relationships and interactions with empathy and critical thinking.

The guilt trip is a tactic used in emotional manipulation where someone tries to make another person feel bad about something they've done or failed to do. The goal is to change their emotional response to the situation, making them feel indebted or guilty. By altering their perception of the situation, the manipulator aims to prompt the person to either correct their behavior or make amends for their mistake.

Here's how it works:

1. Concern about reputation: The person is worried about their reputation. If they gain a reputation as someone who doesn't help others achieve their goals, it could lead to a loss of power. Making amends helps salvage their reputation.

2. Persuasion of severity: The manipulator convinces them of the seriousness of their mistake. This could involve providing genuine new information about the negative impact of their actions or earning enough trust for the person to believe their perspective.
3. Deception: Fabricating details to change their perspective. For example, exaggerating the severity of an injury they caused to someone else. While deception may work in the short term, it's likely to be discovered eventually.
4. Impact of power: The person who made the mistake is affected by the manipulator's power. If the manipulator can remedy the problem, the person is likely to comply with their demands. The more significant they perceive their mistake to be, the greater the manipulator's power over them.

Emotional manipulation comes in various forms, and it's often tricky to distinguish between ethical and unethical practices. For instance, it's hard to pinpoint the boundary between guilt tripping and expressing disappointment since they both involve influencing someone's emotions. Similarly, understanding the difference between intimidation and...

Thankfully, this book isn't delving into these ethical dilemmas just yet. You'll uncover more insights into the ethics of manipulation in the upcoming chapter.

There are many terms for many different types of emotional manipulation. It is not necessary to memorize, or even learn, all of them. By understanding the mechanics of emotional manipulation, you can easily analyze and understand them as they arise. Here are a few examples:

- **Intimidation** – Intimidation is when someone makes another person feel afraid, causing them to change their plans or actions to protect themselves. This can involve the threat of violence, pushing the target to alter their behavior to stay safe, which is a common goal for everyone. The target might comply with the intimidator to ensure their safety, shaping their future actions accordingly.

  It's important to note that the target's response to intimidation isn't necessarily irrational. Emotional manipulation doesn't always lead to irrational behavior. You might notice that intimidation is quite similar to using "the stick" approach.

- **Seduction** – Seduction is when someone manipulates another person by offering them something desirable, but holding it back until they do what the manipulator wants. This desirable thing could be the seducer themselves or something else like money. For example, scam emails promising easy money from Nigerian princes work by tempting the target with the idea of wealth.

Sexual seduction may involve triggering irrational behavior based on the promise of feeling good chemicals called endorphins. Another way to see this is as persuading someone to prioritize a sexual encounter over everything else. Seduction is all about power, as it involves presenting and persuading others with the ability to give them what they desire. You might notice that seduction is quite similar to using "the carrot" approach.

- **Minimization** – Minimization is when someone tries to make an issue or mistake seem less important than it actually is. They might use various manipulation tools like persuasion, deception, or rationalization to downplay the seriousness of the situation.

  For example, they might highlight or even make up facts to show that the problem isn't a big deal. They might also try to explain their actions in a way that makes them seem justified, even if they're not.

  Even though minimization doesn't directly involve power, it's interesting to see how people react differently to this behavior depending on whether the person doing it is seen as powerful or not.

  When someone minimizes a situation, they're essentially trying to make it seem smaller or less significant than it really is. They might do this by emphasizing certain facts or aspects that downplay the seriousness of the issue. For instance, if they made a mistake at work, they might focus on the fact that it didn't cause much harm or that others have made similar mistakes before.

  Persuasion plays a big role in minimization because the person doing it is trying to convince others that the problem isn't as bad as it might seem. They might use words or arguments to sway people's opinions and make them see things from their perspective.

  Deception can also come into play if the person exaggerates or fabricates information to make the situation seem less severe. They might twist the truth or leave out important details to downplay what actually happened.

  Rationalization is another tactic used in minimization. This involves coming up with reasons or excuses to justify their actions or the situation. They might explain why they did what they did in a way that makes it seem acceptable or understandable.

Overall, minimization can be a tricky form of manipulation because it aims to change people's perceptions of a situation rather than their actions directly. It's important to be aware of this tactic and consider the full context before drawing conclusions.

- **Blaming** – Blaming someone else for a mistake or problem is a way to protect yourself and your reputation. It's like shifting the responsibility onto someone else so that you don't look bad. This can be done by convincing others that the other person is actually at fault, or by lying about what really happened.

  Blaming someone else can also be used as a distraction. By making the victim of a situation feel like they're to blame, it can manipulate them into thinking that their reputation is in danger. This can make them more vulnerable to being controlled or manipulated by the person doing the blaming.

  Blaming someone else for a mistake or problem can sometimes be a way to hide the truth or distract attention from oneself. When someone blames a victim, it's like pointing fingers at them and saying it's their fault for what happened. This tactic can make the victim feel scared or insecure about their reputation, so they might do what the blamer wants to avoid further harm. Essentially, it's a way of tricking someone into doing what you want by making them feel guilty or afraid.

Blaming and intimidation go hand in hand, like two sides of the same coin. When someone blames another person, it's like putting pressure on them, either by making them feel guilty or by threatening their reputation. This pressure can change how they behave, either because they feel responsible for what happened or because they're worried about what others might think of them. It's like using fear or the possibility of harm to control someone's actions.

Charisma

Charisma is like a magnetic force that draws people in. It's that special quality that some individuals have, which makes them captivating and influential. While it may seem hard to learn, it's not impossible. Charismatic people have a way of charming others, making them eager to listen and follow their lead. In this book, charisma is highlighted because it's a powerful tool for influencing and manipulating others. Just like a captivating story that keeps you hooked, charisma has the ability to sway opinions and win people over.

Charisma is the illusion of power. And the illusion of power is powerful.

Think of charisma like a spotlight on a stage. Charismatic individuals effortlessly grab that spotlight, shining brightly and captivating everyone's attention. They have a natural magnetism that draws people towards them, like moths to a flame. When they speak, it's like they're casting a spell, holding the audience in their thrall.

But not everyone in powerful positions possesses this innate charm. While some leaders excel at commanding attention and inspiring others, others may struggle to captivate their audience. They might stumble over their words or lack the magnetic presence that draws people in. Yet, despite their lack of natural charisma, they still wield significant influence due to their position or authority.

Even without natural charisma, these leaders can still influence others through different means. They might rely on their expertise, experience, or strategic decision-making to command respect and authority. While they may not shine as brightly on stage, they are still able to steer the direction of their organizations or communities.

In essence, charisma is like a bonus feature that some leaders possess, enhancing their ability to sway opinions and inspire action. However, it's not the only path to power and influence. Leaders can still be effective even without it, as long as they leverage their strengths and capabilities in other areas.

Charisma may not be everything, but it certainly opens doors. It's like a magic cloak that makes you seem more valuable to others, even if they know it's just a show. People expect charismatic individuals to act like talented and smart individuals, so there's a natural connection there. While charisma might not be the real deal, its influence is undeniable.

Charisma can be broken down into two main parts, both essential for its effectiveness:

1. Confidence: Confidence comes from knowing you're capable and experienced. When you appear confident, it gives the impression that you have the skills and know-how to help others achieve their goals.
2. Wit: Wit is like doing mental somersaults. It shows how quick-thinking and mentally agile you are, providing more evidence of your natural abilities and understanding. Being funny adds extra charm.

Imagine someone with confidence but lacking wit. They might end up looking like a fool, constantly bragging without the cleverness to back it up. On the other hand, someone with wit but no confidence, like a silent genius, won't make much of an impact either. Even the cleverest remark won't impress if you don't have the confidence to speak up.

Improving your charisma is like sharpening a blade – it takes time and effort. By building your confidence through gaining knowledge and honing your skills, you lay a solid foundation. Take notes from charismatic individuals, studying how they interact and engage with others to elicit positive responses. Notice how they effortlessly connect with their audience, demonstrating a high level of emotional intelligence. As you progress through this book, you'll learn to analyze others, further enhancing your charisma-building journey.

Additionally, practicing active listening and empathy can enhance your charisma. Just as a painter carefully selects each stroke to create a masterpiece, you can craft your interactions with intention and finesse. By truly understanding and empathizing with others, you'll be able to tailor your approach and connect more deeply. Remember, charisma isn't just about being confident and witty; it's about making genuine connections and leaving a positive impact on those around you.

Charisma is not necessary for manipulation, but it offers a shortcut to power.

Ethical Considerations

If you're not keen on this chapter, you might want to skip ahead.

This chapter dives into the ethical side of manipulation, exploring what's right and wrong within its broad definition. It acknowledges that moral judgments can vary based on culture, laws, religion, and personal beliefs. The goal is to help readers understand the impact of manipulative behavior so they can make informed decisions about their actions.

The exploration of ethics in manipulation serves to provide insight into the consequences of our actions, helping us navigate the complexities of human interaction with greater awareness and responsibility. By understanding the ethical implications, we can strive to engage in behavior that aligns with our values and fosters positive relationships with others.

Understanding the ethical dimensions of manipulation involves considering the impact of our actions on others and recognizing the potential harm that manipulative behavior can cause. It requires introspection and a willingness to evaluate our motives and intentions, as well as the consequences of our actions. By taking a thoughtful approach to manipulation, we can strive to avoid exploiting or harming others for personal gain.

Moreover, exploring ethics in manipulation encourages us to cultivate empathy and compassion in our interactions. It prompts us to consider the perspectives and feelings of those we seek to influence, fostering a more respectful and empathetic approach to communication and persuasion. By prioritizing empathy, we can build stronger and more authentic connections with others, based on mutual understanding and trust.

Ultimately, grappling with ethical questions in manipulation challenges us to strive for integrity and ethical conduct in all aspects of our lives. It prompts us to reflect on our values and principles, and to act in accordance with them, even when faced with temptation or pressure to act otherwise. By upholding ethical standards, we contribute to a more ethical and harmonious social environment, where trust, respect, and integrity prevail.

Deception

If you believe that all forms of lying, even small ones, are morally wrong, then navigating manipulation ethically becomes more challenging. It means you'll need to find alternative strategies that don't rely on deception. Instead, you'll focus more on using your influence and persuasion skills to achieve your goals. While this approach may require more effort and creativity, it ensures that you stay true to your values and maintain integrity in your interactions.

It's Important to acknowledge that everyone has their own moral compass, shaped by their upbringing, beliefs, and experiences. What's considered ethical can vary greatly from person to person. So, while some may see certain manipulative tactics as acceptable or necessary, others may view them as morally unacceptable. Understanding this diversity in perspectives can help you navigate ethical dilemmas more thoughtfully.

For those who don't see lying as universally wrong, it's essential to consider how much and what kinds of deception you're okay with using. This means figuring out where you draw the line and what methods of deception align with your personal values and ethics. It's like deciding which tools you're willing to use in your toolbox of persuasion and manipulation, making sure they match your moral compass.

Deception can have both positive and negative consequences. On one hand, it can lead people to take actions that might not be in their best interest, but benefit the manipulator instead. However, sometimes deception can actually help others, like when it encourages them to do things that are good for their health or career in the long run. For instance, telling a child that their favorite superhero loves vegetables might encourage them to eat healthier, even though they wouldn't have done it otherwise.

Deception, however, can also erode trust and damage relationships. When people discover they've been deceived, it can lead to feelings of betrayal and resentment. This can harm not only the immediate relationship but also future interactions, as trust is difficult to rebuild once it's broken. So, while deception might seem beneficial in the short term, its long-term effects can be detrimental.

In navigating the ethical considerations of deception, it's important to weigh the potential benefits against the possible harm. Sometimes, deception may be justified if it leads to positive outcomes for both parties involved. However, it's crucial to be transparent and considerate of the consequences, ensuring that any deception is for a truly worthwhile cause and doesn't cause unnecessary harm to others.

Deception, even with good intentions, can sometimes lead to unexpected outcomes. While telling a small lie to a child about their favorite superhero enjoying vegetables might seem harmless, there's a chance it could backfire. The child might eventually discover the truth and feel betrayed, leading to a loss of trust in the person who deceived them. This erosion of trust could make the child more wary and suspicious in future interactions, potentially making them more vulnerable to manipulation or even encouraging them to tell lies themselves.

Moreover, the long-term effects of deception on a child's development are uncertain. It's possible that experiencing deception at a young age could influence their attitudes and behaviors in the future. For example, if a child learns that lying can be used to achieve desired outcomes, they might be more inclined to resort to deception themselves in various situations. Alternatively, they might become more skeptical and less trusting of others, which could affect their ability to form healthy relationships later in life.

Ultimately, the consequences of deception are complex and can vary depending on individual circumstances. While it's important to consider the potential benefits of deception, it's equally crucial to weigh them against the possible risks and unintended consequences. Being mindful of the potential impact of deception can help individuals make more informed decisions about when, if ever, it's appropriate to deceive others.

The acceptability of deception often depends on the context in which it occurs. In certain competitive environments, such as games or negotiations, attempting to deceive opponents about one's intentions is not only expected but can also be seen as strategic. For example, in games like chess or contract negotiations, withholding information or misrepresenting one's plans is considered part of the gameplay and is generally accepted. Similarly, in warfare, deception tactics are commonly employed to mislead the enemy and gain an advantage.

However, in personal relationships, particularly those based on trust and intimacy, deception is often viewed as unethical. Many people would consider it immoral to deceive a romantic partner, even about seemingly minor matters. This is because trust is fundamental to the foundation of healthy relationships, and deception can erode that trust, leading to feelings of betrayal and insecurity. Therefore, while deception may be tolerated or even expected in certain competitive or strategic contexts, it is generally frowned upon in personal relationships where honesty and transparency are valued.

Some individuals may adopt a cynical perspective, suggesting that unethical behavior, including deception, is only deemed wrong if one faces consequences or gets caught. This viewpoint reflects a belief in a competitive and ruthless world where individuals prioritize self-interest above all else. In this dog-eat-dog mentality, the argument goes, those unwilling to engage in deceitful tactics risk being taken advantage of by others who are more willing to bend the rules.

However, it's important to recognize that adopting such a perspective comes with ethical implications. While some may justify unethical behavior as a means of self-preservation or success, this mindset can contribute to a culture of mistrust and dishonesty. Furthermore, it overlooks the importance of integrity and moral values in fostering meaningful relationships and building a fair and just society. In essence, it's a matter of personal values and principles, whether one chooses to prioritize short-term gains through deception or uphold ethical standards regardless of the outcomes.

Ultimately, this book does not seek to dictate where individuals should draw their ethical boundaries. Instead, it aims to provide insights into the various forms of manipulation and their potential impacts, allowing readers to make informed decisions about their actions and the ethical considerations involved. By understanding the complexities of manipulation and its consequences, individuals can reflect on their values and navigate moral dilemmas with greater awareness and integrity.

It's advisable to establish personal ethical boundaries, such as refraining from telling lies that have the potential to harm others. This guideline offers a clear standard for evaluating one's actions and decisions, ensuring that ethical considerations are prioritized. However, determining the specifics of these boundaries is a personal endeavor and may vary from individual to individual. Some may find stricter guidelines necessary, while others may opt for more lenient boundaries, depending on their values and beliefs.

By defining and adhering to these ethical boundaries, individuals empower themselves to make conscientious choices in their interactions and decision-making processes. When faced with situations where there's a temptation to compromise these boundaries for personal gain, having a clear ethical framework allows individuals to confront their own morality. This self-awareness enables them to make informed decisions, considering the potential consequences of their actions on others and upholding their personal values and integrity.

Abuse

While this book doesn't dictate your moral compass, it's important to note that most people agree that abuse is wrong. The challenge lies in defining what exactly constitutes abuse.

Abuse can take many forms and may not always be obvious. It can include physical harm, emotional manipulation, verbal aggression, or even neglect. Abuse is about exerting power and control over another person in harmful ways.

Understanding the various forms of abuse and recognizing them is crucial for protecting oneself and others. It's essential to establish clear boundaries and seek help if abuse is suspected or experienced.

The phrase "abuse of power" is commonly heard, and one extreme example is the sexual abuse of mentally handicapped minors. This type of abuse is especially troubling because the minors involved are vulnerable in several ways. They may lack the ability to fully understand or defend themselves against such exploitation.

What makes this form of abuse even more egregious is that the perpetrators often hold positions of trust, such as parents or guardians. These individuals are supposed to protect and care for the minors, but instead, they violate that trust by engaging in harmful behavior. Additionally, the minors may not fully grasp the impact of the abuse on their psychological well-being, making them even more susceptible to harm.

Reflecting on such extreme cases serves as a stark reminder of the gravity of abuse and the importance of protecting vulnerable individuals from exploitation and harm.

On the opposite end of the spectrum, there are more subtle or debatable examples of what some consider abuse. Take, for instance, ordering an extra portion of fries when charging a meal to the company account. It might seem like a small indulgence, but it's an unnecessary extra that allows the person to take advantage of the trust placed in them.

This situation can be likened to taking advantage of a loophole or bending the rules slightly for personal gain. While it may not seem as serious as other forms of abuse, it still involves benefiting unfairly from a position of trust. It's like dipping into the cookie jar when no one's looking, knowing it's not really meant for you.

These actions might not be as extreme as other forms of abuse, but they still undermine the trust and integrity of the system. It's like skirting the edges of what's acceptable, pushing the boundaries without technically breaking any rules. However, it can still be seen as taking advantage of a situation for personal benefit.

In both examples, the common thread is the misuse of trust and power. Whether it's exploiting vulnerabilities in a vulnerable population or taking liberties with company resources, the underlying issue is the abuse of authority. It's important to recognize and address these behaviors to maintain fairness and integrity in all aspects of life.

Taking this even further, it's possible to draw into question the nature of business relationships. You might consider the idea of someone "sleeping their way to the top" to be dismissive. However, how is it possible to reconcile personal relationships where one person clearly has power over the other; for example a boss and an employee, with ideas of the abuse of power? Are these relationships possible without elements of abuse?

A person may naturally be drawn to their boss due to the power they hold, as has been established. At the same time, it may be impossible for a boss to enter into a non-abusive relationship, given the inherent vulnerability of their employee. Perhaps it is completely possible to separate work and pleasure but these situations are sticky, to say the least.

More pertinent to the times, it is possible to draw comparisons to the role of a casting director for Hollywood movies. Many people have said that it is inherently wrong for someone who has power over another, *i.e.* they can help their progress towards achieving their goals, to enter into a romantic relationship. Isn't it the case that, in some of these instances, aspiring actors are throwing themselves at people in positions of power? The implication, then, is that power brings responsibility. Certainly, that carries an element of truth in the eyes of many people and much of the media.

Once again, you will need to decide what constitutes abuse in your eyes. This may be defined by the potential victims of your actions, in which case you might not view a large corporation as a particularly tragic casualty, and order that extra basket of fries. Additional food for thought would be to consider what makes a person "vulnerable" and whether or not it is truly possible to decide that a person is "not vulnerable." If you successfully manipulate another person then, surely, to some degree, they are vulnerable – if only to *your* cunning.

Honor

Navigating all of these ethical issues may, to some degree, force you to rely on a code of honor. This might be dictated by a culture, or a creed. It may be created by yourself or your peers. It may even be part of a commitment made to uphold a certain level of integrity – as is common among reputable media outlets.

This can help you to make ethical decisions, by placing boundaries for you. However, it's rare that, when push comes to shove, a code of honor will actually stop you from taking an action outside of its bounds. That is up you alone.

The Ends Vs The Means

One alternative to establishing clear ethical boundaries is to judge each case completely on its merits. In this instance, there is more flexibility. In particular, you may decide that any action can be justified, if the result is positive enough to outweigh the means of achieving it.

There is a further issue, which even the most flexible moral gymnasts ought to consider. Even if the ends justify the means, could those ends be achieved with less wrongdoing?

Once again, it is not the place of the book to enforce a specific moral code. However, even if your approach to ethics, in manipulation, is flexible, would you lose anything by defining boundaries anyway? At least in that case, you can recognize when you cross those boundaries, and it gives you a prompt to address and justify your reasons for doing so.

Intent and Unscrupulousness

This book has already partly addressed the issue of intent in manipulation. Consider the child who screams; young children make a lot of decisions based on emotion and instinct. The intent may not be to manipulate, but the manipulation is still present.

If you have spent time around children, you may know that, when a child hurts themselves, there is a pause before their reaction. In many cases, they will look to their parent. If the parent's reaction is shock, they may become unsettled and start to cry; if the parent's reaction is to remain calm, often the child will remain calm themselves.

They are learning to navigate the world and their influence within it. It is difficult to assign blame to the child for manipulative behavior, even when you would find such behavior to be unimpressive or undesirable in an adult.

On the subject of adults, you may also differentiate between unscrupulousness (willful disregard for morals or laws that stand in the way of one's goals) and a complete lack of knowledge of those boundaries. Although both are potentially ethical breaches, the latter indicates a lack of responsibility, while the former is an extreme form of egoism – total self-interest.

In practice, this shouldn't be a choice you're able to make. Effective manipulation should involve an analysis of your actions and, at the very least, a reasonable estimate of their results. That means you'll already have the inform

Additionally making moral decisions, based on information and consideration, will allow you to rest in the knowledge that you took responsibility for your decision and actively understood the consequences. It could prevent you from making a decision you live to regret.

The Law

Despite the non-committal nature of this chapter, there is one aspect against which this book advises you completely. That is breaking the law. Under no circumstances is it recommended that you break the law and, if you suspect that you are engaging in criminal activity, including fraud or another form of illegal deception-based manipulation, you are advised to investigate the law thoroughly and avoid any wrongdoing.

Ending up in jail is almost certainly not a way to achieve your goals and the best way to avoid jail is to ***not break the law.***

Methodology

This chapter is where things get really practical. In this chapter, you will learn to apply the ideas established in previous chapters and create an effective strategy for manipulation.

The core of developing an effective manipulation strategy revolves around influencing others to perform actions which further your goals.

Step 1 – Define Your Goal(s)

This is the focus of your manipulation strategy. Without this, you run the risk of manipulating people aimlessly. While diversion *can* be part of an effective manipulation strategy, it should be done deliberately, rather than at random.

One important consideration, regarding your goals, is to determine if they are something you really want to achieve. It's no good saying that your goal is to rule the world, if you aren't willing to put in the effort – who needs that kind of pressure, anyway?

It's also better to define goals, to which there is already a clear path. You may have larger goals, such as becoming the CEO of a Fortune 500 company – however unless you already have a clear idea of your path to that goal, it's probably better to start smaller. Take that goal, and break it down. The first thing you might need is managerial experience.

Give yourself a goal of reaching a managerial position in your company, and have at least 50 people to you, either directly or via the chain of command. Break that down even further, if you need to, and set your first goal as becoming the leader of your team.

Career success isn't the only type of goal this methodology works for. You might set a goal to carve a niche at work which gives you more free time and allows you to work with less stress. You might set a goal to find a loving spouse. The goal itself doesn't matter, as long as you really want it.

Don't forget to set a date on your goal as well. It doesn't matter how you arrive at your estimate – even if you make simple guess – you can always revise it later based on improved information. What a date gives you is a restraint, encouraging you to think creatively in order to accelerate your plans.

Now take a note of all your goals, long-term and short-term, big and small, and order them in terms of immediacy.

Remind yourself of your goals every single day.

In doing so, you are focusing your brain on a task. Think of a time when achieved highly at work, school or college. Think about what it took to achieve something that made you proud. Was it working a moderate amount of hours or did it involve going the extra mile? Were you thinking about the project night and day, running it through in your head before you went to sleep and structuring it in your mind? Of course you were. That's what made the difference.

By focusing your brain on a task, you dedicated all your resources to achieving highly. The more attention you dedicated to manipulation, the more you'll be able to accomplish and the better you'll succeed at it.

Oh and keep your goals a secret from everyone for now, naturally.

Step 2 – Map Out Your Paths to Success

Now that you have your goals, and you've broken them down sufficiently, it should be fairly easy to find a path to success. If your goal is a promotion, you'll need a boss to promote you. If your goal is finding a loving spouse, you'll need to find someone who's going to provide that and for them to agree to marriage.

Consider alternate paths to success as well. For instance, if you want to take your boss' position, one path might be for them to get fired, leaving a vacancy for you. In another situation, they could be promoted, leaving a spot open.

Map out as many paths as you can and consider them all possibilities for now.

Once you've done that, it's time to establish the parties involved. Who would be in charge of the decision-making process for your promotion? Who are your potential rivals? How does information flow between these people?

In the case of achieving a promotion, your manipulation strategy should be to make the people, who have the power to promote you, *want* to do so. You've seen the movie *Inception*, right? Unfortunately hacking into someone's dreams isn't an option.

In order to manipulate *your* target, you need to start understanding their goals and behavior.

Step 3 – Gather Information

This book's final chapters will directly address analyzing people, including yourself. For now, it is enough to include it as part of your manipulation strategy.

Consider the goals of the people whom you need to influence – those who will decide whether or not you are promoted. Map out all of their actions, starting from now and as much of their previous behavior as possible. Look for patterns and attempt to relate each of their actions to what you perceive as their goals. Then look for ways in which they don't align and reassess their goals to see pinpoint what matches.

Make an assessment of your own assets. Include hard facts, such as your time at a company, your currently salary and your qualifications, as well as soft skills, such as charisma and persuasion.

Profile all the parties involved, including those who have the power to promote you, your rivals and anyone in orbit of your path to success. Include their goals and try to record their actions, spotting patterns and connecting them to their goals. Keep organized notes of all of this information and conceal it from *everyone*.

The aim here is to give your brain as much information as possible. Once again, imagine your brain as a machine. It has the best chance of producing the correct outputs (actions) if it has access to the best inputs (information) and the better you can objectively organize this information, the easier it will be to make smart decisions, rather than subjective decisions based on instinct.

After a while, say a few days, you should start to build a picture. Take more time if you feel like you need it. However, you don't need to have a perfect understanding of the situation to begin the next stage of information gathering, which is to identify key figures among those who you are profiling and start doing the same thing for people related to *their* goals. In the case of those who have the power to promote you, this may very well be the people who have the power to promote *them*.

Going a step further is going to give you an even deeper understanding of the way that these people operate, what drives them and what is likely to impact their decisions.

You will continue gathering information indefinitely, even as you begin manipulating others. Make it a habit and you will get better at identifying the goals and behavioral patterns of others faster and more accurately.

Focus on understanding where power lies and how the parties involved reach their decisions – try to identify what provokes them to take certain actions.

Relate this back to their own goals.

Step 4 – Identify Opportunities and Threats

the moment to engage your intellect fully. It's time to immerse yourself in your goals every single day, gaining a deeper grasp of how your situation works. Think of it like tending to a garden, where each day you nurture your plants with care and attention, ensuring they grow strong and healthy. Similarly, with your goals, consistent attention and understanding will help them flourish.

Picture your mind as a workshop, where you carefully craft your plans and strategies. Each day, you refine your understanding of your goals, honing your skills like a master craftsman perfecting their masterpiece. Just as a skilled artisan meticulously shapes each piece of their creation, you shape your future with thoughtful consideration and precision.

So, keep your mind sharp and focused, like a sculptor chiseling away at a block of marble to reveal the masterpiece within. Every thought and action you take brings you closer to your goals, much like each stroke of the sculptor's tool brings them closer to revealing the beauty hidden within the stone.

Opportunities

Let's break down what you've discovered about the goals of the decision-makers who hold the key to your promotion. Suppose they aim to boost the team's profitability, emphasizing the importance of increasing efficiency to achieve higher profits. Understanding their objectives is like unlocking a door to their motivations and priorities. It's akin to uncovering the Treasure map leading to success, where each piece of information reveals a clue about their desired destination.

Now, armed with this knowledge, you can assess the likelihood of success in different scenarios. For instance, consider whether your current team leader will be promoted or replaced. Reflect on whether there are alternative paths to advancement within or outside the company. It's like being a skilled navigator, carefully charting the course through uncertain waters, weighing the risks and rewards of each potential route to your destination.

Ultimately, the key lies in evaluating the options available and choosing the path that aligns best with your goals and the interests of those in power. Just as a skilled captain navigates through stormy seas to reach the desired port, you too must navigate the currents of corporate dynamics to steer your career towards success. By leveraging your understanding of the decision-makers' objectives, you can plot a course that maximizes your chances of reaching your destination.

Imagine you suspect that your current team leader isn't meeting expectations and could be on the verge of being let go. It's like sensing a storm brewing on the horizon. In such a situation, timing is crucial. You must be ready to seize the moment when the opportunity arises, much like a skilled surfer catching the perfect wave. Being in pole position means being in the best possible position to take advantage of the situation when it unfolds.

Being in pole position means being prepared and positioned strategically to capitalize on the unfolding events. It's akin to being the first in line at a race, poised to sprint ahead when the starting gun fires. So, if you foresee a change in leadership, ensure you're ready to step up and demonstrate your capabilities when the time is right. Just like a vigilant sailor who adjusts the sails to catch the wind at the opportune moment, be ready to navigate the shifting currents of the workplace to your advantage.

What if you're in pole position right now? Then it's time to get your team leader fired as soon as possible.

Relate this to the three main tools of manipulation identified in earlier chapters:

- Power – As the candidate in pole position, you are perceived to have the most power to help your *potential* new bosses (those who would promote you) to achieve their goals. Likewise, you have also identified that your current boss, your team-leader, is facing the chop. This is, almost certainly, because they are perceived to *lack* the power to help their immediate superiors achieve their goals. However, they haven't been fired yet. This might be for a number of reasons. Perhaps they haven't had enough opportunity to prove themselves. Perhaps their superiors aren't certain about you as a replacement.
- Persuasion – Forget marching up to those with the power to promote you and giving an epic speech about why you're the

perfect candidate to be the next team-leader. This isn't a Hollywood movie. More to the point, the world won't simply bend to your knees because you ask it to.

- Deception – What you *can* do is act to control the flow of information that reaches your boss' superiors. The aim, in this instance, is to decrease their perception of your boss' power and get your boss fired more quickly.

The ways in which you could achieve this are too many to list. How close are you to these people, whom you need to influence? Who has their ear and what makes them tick? Perhaps another team-leader, reliant on the actions of your team, is likely to complain about your boss if your team fails to deliver.

Now think: who has *their* ear? Possibly someone on their team. Possibly someone with whom you're on talking terms. Now you have an opportunity, sufficiently distanced from yourself, to indirectly influence the people directly above your boss.

Recapping, this refers to someone, of roughly your level, working for a team, roughly the same level as your own, which is dependent on the actions of your team. Immediately begin profiling this person, their goals and their actions.

Bear in mind, this is a hypothetical example, but it gives you the idea of the kind of person you might stand to gain by influencing. You will have to analyze your own situation and form a strategy based on these ideas.

Note that so much of what goes into effective manipulation is deciding *who* to manipulate. You are likely to be manipulating everyone at once, to some degree. Later chapters will give you advice on how to project power using body language and speech, giving you increased opportunities for manipulation in general. Right now, you are forming a strategy for manipulating a specific situation through extraordinary means.

Threats

A threat, in this instance, is any rival who has the potential to be promoted ahead of you. An additional threat is your boss recovering their reputation (perceived power) and getting out of the danger-zone. Consider anything, which can serve to disrupt your path to success, as a potential threat.

Look for threats constantly and use the same principles to thwart them. Specifically, act covertly to reduce the power of any parties which threaten to disrupt your plans.

Step 5 – Take Action

Leaving threats aside, refocus on the current example. Here, an opportunity has presented itself to create a deception. It may well be the case that you have a close relationship with the person identified to start the flow information, in which case it might be possible to conspire. If your boss is truly useless, and your target's team is truly dependent on an improvement in your team's performance, *and* your target aims to see that happen, you could *theoretically* agree to work together, in order to perpetuate some information that will damage the reputation of your boss.

But take a moment to look at some of the risks:

- Your collaborator is another person who can be discovered and the conspiracy could come back to you.
- You have revealed to another person that you wish to conspire. This will have an effect on their opinion of you, and your trustworthiness.
- Your collaborator may change their mind, in which case you will have sabotaged your chance to deceive them by revealing your goals.
- Your collaborator may alter the plan to suit their own goals and compromise your strategy.

With deception, you only run the risk of being found out yourself and it's quite possible to attempt a deception with plausible deniability.

For the purposes of this example, say you are on friendly terms with this person and may eat lunch or take coffee with them roughly once a week. Show an active interest by asking them questions. Mix in questions about their work with a normal, personal interest in the person. Try to focus on pursuing lines of conversation about which they're willing to talk. There is a good chance this will relate to their interests, which will relate to their goals.

Look for something in their goals which is affected by your boss' actions. Say their team handles delivery, while your team handles production. This is a simple paradigm, given that the example relies on their team's dependence on yours. Establish the issues facing delivery and analyze elements of your boss' behavior which could be revealed, in order for your target to arrive at the conclusion your boss is bad news. This could be a tendency to ignore the demands of shipping when forming a production schedule.

It's important not to do this at a time when your target is specifically talking about their issues. You should also reveal the information in such a way that does not arouse suspicion. For example, when a natural opportunity arises, you might explain the way your boss scheduled production, which clearly illustrates the absence of shipping.

At this point, the example has reached such a degree of specificity, that it is almost certainly impossible to directly relate to your circumstances. You will always need to look for opportunities specific to your own situation when engaging in manipulation. This will require you to act ingeniously, by giving yourself as much information as possible.

You have now planted the seed of an idea in your target's head. Your boss is having a negative impact on your target's professional success due to their methods. In the eyes of your target, the goals of your boss fail to align with their own. They must go. You have recruited someone to do your bidding, without arousing suspicion. You have maintained a normal co-worker relationship but achieved a deception by actively controlling the flow of information to those who have power over your future.

If all goes according to plan, the next time your co-worker falls behind in their work or struggles to make a deadline, they'll know exactly who to blame. Their team leader will relay this information to their superiors and your boss will become even more of a problem than before, edging closer to their professional doom.

Step 6 – Learn and Improve

Unfortunately, your plan has every chance of failure. It might be that your boss manages production in the way they do for an important reason – one which might be recognized by their superiors. In that case, it could even backfire. But at least you weren't rumbled. Take note from this manipulation attempt and use it to inform your future efforts.

There is no way to predict the future perfectly but looking at the past is the best way to get an approximation. Use the ideas of this methodology to develop your own strategies and manipulate the world around you for your own ends.

Analysis

This chapter connects back to ideas discussed in the previous chapter about how manipulation works. It's like tracing a path back to where you started on a map, seeing how each step leads to the next. Just as each step in a journey builds upon the last, each chapter in this book builds upon the concepts introduced earlier.

Think of it as laying the foundation for a house. Each chapter adds another layer of bricks, reinforcing the structure and making it stronger. Similarly, each new concept introduced in this chapter builds upon the framework established in the previous one, creating a comprehensive understanding of manipulation tactics.

So, as you delve into this chapter, remember to draw upon the knowledge you gained from the previous one, like adding pieces to a puzzle until the picture becomes clear. By connecting the dots between chapters, you'll gain a deeper insight into the methodology behind manipulation.

you'll dive into methods of analysis, which essentially means learning how to study and understand the people who hold the power to either support or hinder your goals. It's like studying a chessboard to anticipate your opponent's next move. By analyzing their behavior and actions, you can better predict their intentions and strategize accordingly.

Practice plays a crucial role in mastering this skill. It's like honing your skills in a sport or musical instrument – the more you practice observing behaviors and predicting actions, the better you become at it. Think of it as sharpening a blade to make it more effective in cutting through obstacles. With each observation and prediction, you refine your understanding and increase your accuracy.

However, don't be discouraged by initial failures. Every mistake is an opportunity to learn and improve. It's like stumbling while learning to ride a bike – each fall teaches you something new about balance and control.

Reflect on why your prediction didn't pan out as expected and use that insight to adjust your approach in the future. Over time, you'll naturally become more skilled at analyzing and predicting outcomes.

So, embrace the process of learning and practicing analysis. It's like planting seeds in a garden – with patience, diligence, and care, you'll nurture your skills and watch them grow into powerful tools for achieving your goals.

Self-Analysis

A great way to get started in understanding how others act and what they're after is by looking at yourself first. Imagine you're watching a movie, but the main character is you. Take note of everything you do, like a detective gathering clues. Pay attention to why you do things, especially whether they move you closer to your goals or hold you back.

Think of it like being both the scientist and the subject in an experiment. You're observing your own behavior with a curious eye, trying to uncover the patterns and motivations behind what you do. By doing this, you'll gain valuable insights into how your actions influence your success.

It's similar to peeling back the layers of an onion. Each observation you make about yourself reveals something new, helping you understand yourself better. And as you become more aware of your own motivations and behaviors, you'll be better equipped to understand and predict the actions of others.

What you're aiming for is to be as objective as possible, like seeing things from an impartial viewpoint. This helps you make wise choices about your future. It's important to notice that we're talking about making "good" decisions here. You might already be making decisions that make sense, but that doesn't guarantee they're the best ones for you.

Think of it like being a judge in a courtroom, weighing all the evidence before making a verdict. You want to gather all the facts and consider them carefully before deciding what to do next. That way, you're more likely to steer yourself in the right direction.

Imagine you're navigating through a maze, but you're not sure which paths lead to treasure and which lead to dead ends. Sometimes, you might pick a direction that seems right, but it ends up being a wrong turn because you didn't have all the information. Similarly, in life, you might be making choices based on what you think is best, but if you don't have a clear understanding of what really works in your favor, you might end up going in circles.

By gaining more knowledge and looking at things from a neutral standpoint, like getting a bird's-eye view of the maze, you can start to see the patterns more clearly. This helps you figure out which paths are worth exploring and which ones you should avoid. In the end, it's about arming yourself with the right information so you can navigate through life's twists and turns more effectively.

Think of your instincts as the little voice inside your head that speaks up when something doesn't feel quite right. It's like having a built-in alarm system that alerts you when you're about to face a challenge or a danger. Pay attention to what triggers that instinctive response in you. Is it a certain situation, person, or even a specific word? Understanding what sets off your instincts can help you anticipate and prepare for similar situations in the future.

Sometimes, our instincts can lead us astray, causing us to make decisions that don't serve us well. It's like having a faulty compass that occasionally points us in the wrong direction. Reflect on times when you've acted impulsively or made decisions that didn't make sense in hindsight. By analyzing these moments, you can uncover patterns and triggers that prompt you to act irrationally. This awareness allows you to pause and reconsider before jumping into action.

Ultimately, by examining both your rational thinking and your instincts, you gain a more complete understanding of yourself and how you respond to the world around you. It's like piecing together a puzzle to see the bigger picture of who you are and why you react the way you do. Armed with this knowledge, you can make more informed decisions and navigate life's challenges with greater clarity and confidence.

Think of self-analysis as holding up a mirror to your actions and behaviors. It's like taking a step back to observe yourself from an outsider's perspective. By doing this, you can spot moments when your decisions have a negative impact on your reputation and influence. For example, if you react impulsively or lose control in a situation, others may perceive you as unreliable or unstable, diminishing your power in their eyes.

Imagine yourself as the captain of a ship navigating through stormy waters. When the seas are rough, it's tempting to let panic take over and steer erratically. However, a skilled captain knows that maintaining composure and staying focused on charting the right course is crucial for reaching safe harbor. Similarly, in life's challenges, controlling your immediate reaction is key to preserving your power and influence.

Remember, every action you take sends a message to the world about who you are and what you stand for. Just like a master chess player carefully considers each move before making it, you too should pause and assess the situation before acting. Rushing into decisions without understanding the full scope of the situation can often lead to unfavorable outcomes and weaken your position.

In essence, self-analysis empowers you to take control of your reactions and make decisions that serve your long-term goals. It's like being the architect of your own destiny, shaping your path with intention and foresight. By cultivating self-awareness and practicing restraint when necessary, you can navigate life's challenges with grace and resilience, emerging stronger and more powerful than before.

Identifying your own impulsive instincts not only helps you understand yourself better but also offers valuable insights into the motivations of others. When people react impulsively, it often indicates that their power or the likelihood of achieving their goals is being challenged. By observing these reactions in yourself and others, you can gain a deeper understanding of what drives people's actions and behaviors.

Imagine you're a detective unraveling clues to solve a mystery. Each impulsive action taken by others is like a piece of evidence that helps you piece together the puzzle of their intentions and desires. By empathizing with people in these moments, you can step into their shoes and see the world from their perspective. This empathetic approach allows you to grasp the underlying motivations behind their impulsive behavior.

Just as a skilled tracker reads the signs left by animals to understand their movements and habits, you can decipher the signals of human behavior to uncover hidden motives and goals. Through self-analysis and empathy, you become adept at interpreting the subtle cues that reveal people's inner drives and aspirations. Armed with this understanding, you can navigate social interactions more effectively and forge stronger connections with others.

Analyzing Others

Along with empathy, using your self-analysis and lived experience to place yourself in the shoes of others, you can also recognize the behavioral patterns of other objectively.

The introduction to this chapter offers a nice summary. Here is an opportunity to present the process of analyzing others in a more systematic manner:

1. Begin by observing and recording every action that a person takes. Provide yourself with as much data as possible. Include every unusual mood, action, reaction and impulse.
2. Hypothesize obvious and suspected goals which that person many possess.
3. Test their actions in relation to these goals. Try to understand if the person is acting to achieve these goals, in which case your hypothesized goals are correct, or if the actions and your hypothesized goals fail to align, in which case you may need to consider that the person is pursuing alternative goals.
4. Predict the actions of a person, based on their goals and the behavioral patterns (patterns in the actions they take) you observe. Specifically, when something unusual occurs, try to predict how they will react. Analyze your success and failures in prediction. Where you fail, try to understand why the person reacted as they did, why you failed to predict that and use it to inform your future predictions.
5. Repeat steps 3 and 4 ad infinitum, until you can accurately predict the behavior of that person.

With this ability to predict the reaction of a person to a given event, it only requires your creativity to reverse-engineer an event based on the reaction you wish to produce. The event might be as simple and innocent as mentioning a certain topic of conversation, revealing a piece of information or thanking them for some work they've done.

Cold Reading

Cold reading is like being a detective who can quickly size up a person just by looking at them. It's a handy skill because it lets you influence someone's thoughts or actions even in a brief encounter. By observing subtle clues in their behavior, appearance, and mannerisms, you can make surprisingly accurate predictions about how they will respond to certain situations.

Think of cold reading as decoding a secret message hidden in someone's words and actions. Like a codebreaker deciphering a cryptic message, you analyze their gestures, facial expressions, and speech patterns to uncover their hidden motivations and desires. With this insight, you can tailor your approach to steer the conversation in a direction that serves your purpose.

Mastering the art of cold reading is like having a superpower that allows you to anticipate people's next moves before they even make them. It's about reading between the lines and understanding the unsaid thoughts and emotions that drive human behavior. With practice, you can become adept at influencing others subtly and achieving your desired outcomes with ease.

Cold reading is something we all do without even realizing it. It's like making a guess about a book just by looking at its cover. We often form quick judgments about people based on superficial factors like how they dress, their facial expressions, or even their accent. These snap judgments are like taking a wild guess at solving a puzzle without all the pieces.

However, relying solely on appearances for understanding someone is like trying to solve a mystery with incomplete clues. Just because someone dresses a certain way or speaks with a particular accent doesn't mean we know everything about them. People are complex, and there's often more to them than meets the eye. It's like trying to predict the ending of a movie based on the first few scenes – you might be completely off track.

While cold reading can provide some insight into a person, it's far from foolproof. It's like trying to navigate a maze blindfolded – you might stumble upon the right path occasionally, but more often than not, you'll end up lost. People are full of surprises, and relying solely on surface-level observations can lead to misunderstandings and missed opportunities for genuine connection.

Improving your cold reading skills is like sharpening a tool in your toolkit. It takes practice and patience. When you meet new people, try making predictions about them based on your initial impressions. Maybe jot down these predictions or memorize them quickly. It's like gathering puzzle pieces to solve a mystery. As you interact more with the person, pay attention to whether your predictions were accurate or not. This is like testing your theories to see if they hold true.

Reflecting on your cold reading attempts is like reviewing your notes after a challenging lesson. Think about whether there were any subtle cues you missed or misinterpreted. It's like going back to study a tricky problem to understand where you went wrong. By analyzing your findings and comparing them to your initial impressions, you can identify patterns and improve your accuracy over time. It's like refining your strategy in a game to increase your chances of winning.

Remember, effective cold reading isn't about making wild guesses or jumping to conclusions. It's about observing, analyzing, and adjusting based on new information. Think of it like navigating a maze – each new piece of information is like a clue guiding you towards understanding the bigger picture. With practice and reflection, you can become more adept at deciphering the complexities of human behavior.

Body Language

Body language is useful as both a source of information, and an approach to manipulation. It can form a part of both deception *and* persuasion.

You have probably heard quotes like "body language makes up 55% of all communication," before. Although the number, "55%," is actually pretty useless, the message remains clear that body language is an important part of the way people communicate to one another.

Considering the fact that body language is so important, it's no surprise that everyone is able to read body language and react to it, to some degree. On a subconscious level, you can probably already understand when someone disagrees with what you are saying, or is interested, or just wants to stop talking to you altogether. These cues are intended to be understood – without that, there would be no point to their existence.

However, there are important ways to read the body language of others, which can help you to analyze their intentions, even when they are attempting to deceive you.

Facial Expressions

It's a famous poker trope that everyone has a particular behavior which they exhibit when "bluffing," a form of deception intended to lead opponent players to believe they have a stronger hand than they actually do. This is known as a "tell."

While there is some truth to this, and you may be able to spot giveaway signs to recognize when a person is lying. However, this will be limited in accuracy and, particularly in the poker, you might fall prey to a deception, in which someone is deliberately putting on a tell, in order to throw you off the scent.

In reality, facial expressions tend to be extremely unreliable when determining if someone is telling the truth or not. They are easy to fake and don't offer much in the way of help when it comes to analyzing others.

However, as a tool for manipulation, facial expressions happen to be somewhat useful. One general tip is to give people a big eyebrow raise and light up your face with interest upon greeting people. Most people greet one another with stern professionalism – it's such an easy tip but raising your eyebrows and smiling at someone can create a lasting impression. There's no need to be obsequious; don't coo or gaze. Just show comfort, confidence and a project a genuinely positive reaction from seeing someone.

The power of positivity indicates to others that you have a willingness to be constructive and helpful to others. People crave the influence of positive people, as a positive attitude breeds achievement.

Reading Body Language

So, if the face is limited in reading the non-verbal communicative cues of a person, where should you look? The answer happens to be relatively simple: the feet.

Most people reflect their desire and their attention by pointing their feet. If you sense something off about a conversation, and get the feeling someone would like to be somewhere else, glance at their feet and, if they're pointing towards the door, there's your clincher.

Naturally, you don't want to spend all your time staring at someone's feet. But take a glance and use their position to recognize whether someone wants to be in the conversation or not. If they're pointing right at you, they're likely to be a lot more receptive to what you're saying.

If they're pointing away from you, it's possible you might as well be talking to a brick wall. Now, the reason for that can vary. It doesn't necessarily mean they don't like you; they might just be late for another appointment or have other things on their mind. You need to use your learned analysis and incorporate body language to form a complete picture.

Thank you for engaging with the content. Now equipped with potent techniques, you hold a powerful tool in your hands. Utilize this knowledge wisely and thoughtfully, like a skilled craftsman wielding a finely honed instrument.

Sincerely,

Pankaj Tiwari